All this helps to increase observation, and speech and reading vocabulary.

Friends will enjoy reading the hymns to each other or together, and all will enjoy bringing their own hymn books to assembly each morning.

It is a good idea to have a hymn board hung where the children can refer to it. This should give the number and first line of the hymn, thus giving practice in recognizing the words and numbers.

Tunes are left to the choice of the school.

To our dear "granddaughter"
Darlene Rand
From "Pop-pop" Anthony
in Florida

Christmas 1977

A Ladybird First book of
HYMNS AND SONGS

compiled by IRENE DARK

with illustrations by A. N. BUCHANAN

REVISED EDITION 1969

Publishers: Ladybird Books Ltd . Loughborough
© Ladybird Books Ltd (formerly Wills & Hepworth Ltd) 1968
Printed in England

All things bright and beautiful,
All creatures great and small,
All things wise and wonderful,
The Lord God made them all.

He gave us eyes to see them,
And lips that we might tell
How great is God Almighty
Who hath made all things well.

0 7214 0227 5

Away in a manger,
No crib for a bed,
The little Lord Jesus
Laid down His sweet head.
The stars in the bright sky
Looked down where He lay,
The little Lord Jesus
Asleep on the hay.

Do no sinful action,
Speak no angry word.
You belong to Jesus,
Children of the Lord.

Christ was kind and gentle,
Christ was pure and true,
And His little children
Must be holy too.

Down the air
Everywhere
God is sending rain,
Dropping, dropping,
Dropping, dropping,
Down the window pane.
Pitter, patter,
Pitter, patter,
Down the window pane.
Pitter, patter,
Pitter, patter,
Thank God for the rain.

Father we thank Thee
             for the night,
And for the pleasant
             morning light,
For rest and food,
             and loving care,
And all that makes the day
             so fair.
Help us to do the things
             we should,
To be to others kind and good,

In all we do, at work, or play,

To grow more loving every day.

For butterflies and bees,
For singing birds and trees,
For flowers and wind and sun,
We thank God, everyone.

For food, and clothes and fun,
For strength to walk and run,
For home, and school and friends,
Our song of thanks ascends.

Glad that I live am I,
That the sky is blue,
Glad for the country lanes
And the fall of dew.
After the sun, the rain,
After the rain, the sun,
This is the way of life
Till the work be done.
All that we need to do,
Be we low or high,
Is to see that we grow
Nearer the sky.

God always listens
Whenever we pray.
He's never too busy
To hear what we say.
So we will say, "Thank you"
For what each day brings,
Children to play with
And many good things.

God Who made the earth,
The air, the sky, the sea,
Who gave the light its birth,
Careth for me.

God Who made the grass,
The flower, the fruit, the tree,
The day and night to pass,
Careth for me.

God, Whose name is Love,
Happy children we,
Listen to the hymn
That we sing to Thee.

Help us to be good,
Always kind and true,
In the games we play
Or the work we do.

Jesus bids us shine
With a pure, clear light,
Like a little candle
Burning in the night.
In this world of darkness
We must shine,
You in your small corner
And I in mine.

Jesus bids us shine, then
For all around.
Many kinds of darkness
In this world are found.
Sin, and want, and sorrow,
So we must shine,
You in your small corner
And I in mine.

Heavenly Father, hear my prayer:
Night and day I'm in Thy care;
Look upon me from above,
Bless the home I dearly love;
Bless the friends with whom I
                        play,
Make us kinder day by day.

Jesus loves me, this I know,
For the Bible tells me so.
Little ones to Him belong,
They are weak, but He is strong.
Yes, Jesus loves me,
Yes, Jesus loves me,
Yes, Jesus loves me,
The Bible tells me so.

Boys and girls across the sea,
Jesus loves, as well as me,
So our little friends are they
And with us they all can say,
"Yes, Jesus loves me,
Yes, Jesus loves me,
Yes, Jesus loves me,
The Bible tells me so."

Little bird, I have heard
What a merry song you sing,
Soaring high to the sky
On your tiny wing.

Jesu's little lambs are we,
And He loves us, you and me,
As we share in His care
We must happy be.

All the day, lambs at play
In the fields where daisies grow,
Skip about, in and out,
They are happy so.

Now the day is over,
Night is drawing nigh,
Shadows of the evening
Steal across the sky.

Now the darkness gathers,
Stars begin to peep,
Birds and beasts and flowers
Soon will be asleep.

Once in royal David's city,
Stood a lowly cattle shed,
Where a mother laid her baby,
In a manger for His bed.
Mary was that mother mild,
Jesus Christ her little child.

He came down to earth
                        from heaven,
Who is God and Lord of all,
And His shelter was a stable,
And His cradle was a stall.
With the poor, and meek
                        and lowly,
Lived on earth our Saviour holy.

Over the earth is a mat of
                              green,
Over the green, the dew,

Over the dew, the arching
                              trees,
Over the trees, the blue.

Across the blue are
                    scudding clouds,
Over the clouds, the sun,

Over the sun is the love of
                              God,
Blessing us everyone.

Praise Him, praise Him,
All His little children,
He is love, He is love.
Praise Him, praise Him
All His little children,
He is love, He is love.

Thank Him, thank Him,
All His little children,
He is love, He is love.
Thank Him, thank Him,
All His little children,
He is love, He is love.

Sing a song of springtime,
Sing a song of spring.
Flowers are in their beauty,
Birds are on the wing.
Springtime, springtime,
God has given us springtime.
Thank Him for His gift of love,
Thank Him for the spring.

Tell me the stories of Jesus
I love to hear.
Things I would ask Him to tell me
If He were here.
Scenes by the wayside,
Tales of the sea,
Stories of Jesus,
Tell them to me.

Winter day, frosty day!
God a cloak on all doth lay:
On the earth the snow He
                  sheddeth
O'er the lamb a fleece He
                  spreadeth,
Gives the bird a coat of feather,
To protect it from the weather.
Gives the children home and
                  food,
Let us praise Him; God is good.

Twinkle, twinkle little star,
How I wonder what you are,
Up above the world so high,
Like a diamond in the sky.
Twinkle, twinkle little star
How I wonder what you are.

We plough the fields and scatter
The good seed on the land,
But it is fed and watered
By God's almighty hand.
He sends the snow in winter,
The warmth to swell the grain,
The breezes and the sunshine
And soft, refreshing rain.

All good gifts around us
Are sent from Heaven above,
Then thank the Lord
O thank the Lord
For all His love.

When lamps are lighted
in the town,
The boats sail out to sea.

The fishers watch when
night comes down,
They work for you and me.

We little children go to rest.

Before we sleep, we pray

That God will bless
the fishermen
And bring them back at day.